JENNISODES PRESENTS:
PROJECT
NINJA PANDA TACO

GAME DESIGNER
Jennifer Steen

EDITOR
John Adamus

ILLUSTRATOR
Brian Patterson

LAYOUT ARTIST
Daniel Solis

Jennisodes

DEDICATION AND THANK YOU

This game is dedicated to my loving husband and two
puppies who have supported me in all my gaming adventures.
Also, Tacos, Pandas, Puppies, Dice, Gaming.

A special thanks to Cassie Krause for her assistance with the
classroom play section, to Luke Crane for his encouragement
and guidance, and to John, Brian and Daniel for their amazing
talents and support.

TABLE OF CONTENTS

OVERVIEW

PROJECT NINJA PANDA TACO
is a collaborative story-telling game where each player, acting as a Mastermind, attempts to take over the world, while preventing their Nemesis from doing the same while Minions help whoever gives them the best loot. This game is outlandish, zany, megalomaniacal and perfect for any age.

Any Mastermind can try to take over the world but only the smartest and most creative succeed. The Masterminds always need some help to pull off their plan so they ask Minions for help. Minions love to help, and love to receive items for helping, but Minions are also incredibly simple-minded, and may not always help a particular plan succeed.

Enter the world of the Masterminds and find out how you will take over the world.

THINGS YOU NEED TO PLAY

4 to 6 players

8 fudge dice - 4 of one color and 4 of another

2 tokens per player - Each token is a different color. Tokens can be chips, stones, or coins.

3 note cards per player

Character Sheet for each player

INTRODUCTION

WELCOME THE WORLD OF THE MASTERMINDS

My name is Mastermind Kentucky McCoy and you must be here to find out how to become like me. I reckon I'm the most powerful Mastermind in the world, and I'm guessing that's what you want to be too. This world here is like a rodeo for those who try to rule it. One minute you are on top of the world and the next you are thrown off, just like riding a buckin' bronco.

Look around. You may be wondering where all these other mighty fine Masterminds come from. We each belong to the International League of Masterminds, hidden here in the most secure of secret locations.

I remember the day when I became a Mastermind. I rode up to the International League of Masterminds on a Tuesday evening, I think it was. The head Mastermind, Mastermind Princess Fontina, strapped on this here shiny Mastermind pin. You can see it right here pinned to the lapel of my purple leather jacket. I hope you're ready to strap on your boots and get going, time's a-wastin'.

You look like the type of person that can stand up to a challenge. Part of being a mastermind is that you must come up with a three-step plan to take over the world. You look mighty confused so let me tell you about mine. My plan was called Project Puppy Lemon Waffle Iron. I remember it fondly...

First I lassoed all the puppies in the world and created the cutest 24-hour television show full of puppies. Everyone in the world watched it and become so obsessed with the show they did everything I said. It was nice.

In the second part of Project Puppy Lemon Waffle Iron, I sold lemons to everyone in the world, collecting all of the monies... all of them. I know you are probably thinking that I'm off my rocker but it really did work. Once I collected all of the monies I gave half to the Minions who helped me. It's always nice to give the Minions some pretty little thing – they live for getting stuff.

For the last part of my plan I made the biggest waffle iron the world has ever seen!

Then with all of the monies, all of them... well half of the monies, I was able to create the largest waffle that anyone had ever seen.

My plan to take over the world has been talked about for ages now. It really was a masterpiece.

Being a Mastermind may look easier than milking a cow but there is a downside. Every Mastermind has a Nemesis. Have you ever wondered why all your left socks have holes in them or why that chicken crossed the road? It's because a Mastermind's plan got thwarted by his Nemesis. They are the Yang to your Yin, the humidity to your good hair day. They're the white shoes to your Labor Day. They're the 8-track to your mp3 collection ooh, they just make me so mad.

My Nemesis is Mastermind Dark Baron Harold Siegfried with his darn telekinetic hard hat. He must be everyone's Nemesis because no one liked him. He was constantly trying to ruin my plan to take over the world with his silly hat. He almost succeeded when we were on top of a volcano in Hawaii. I don't know what came of him after he fell into the volcano but I reckon he put his secret lair there, you know because he likes clichés.

I hope he doesn't come back to stop my next plan.

There is one more element of world dominatin' that will leave you grinning like a weasel in a hen house. These here are mighty fine fellows called Minions. They love to help the Masterminds such as yourself complete whatever plan you're thinkin' of doin'. All you have to do is promise them a new item for their tool belt and they will be ready faster than lickety-split.

If you look yonder you can see my favorite Minion right there. His name is Minion Walter Pantaloons and he has many items on his tool belt. He sure has been helpful. As you can see all the Minions have a nametag. Fortunately they all belong to Minion Union 1525 that meets in the basement of the International League of Masterminds. The basement isn't all that bad, we keep it stocked with grub and drinks.

I hear that down there the Minions like to show off their shiny new tool belt items. They talk about their latest plan they assisted in and laugh about how a Mastermind failed.

Just to let you know - having the most toolbelt items is something those wee little Minions get very competitive about. Like this time Walter helped me with the world's largest waffle iron, he gloated about his lifetime supply of syrup for WEEKS. He talked about it constantly. Especially on the Facebook.

You've been mighty kind to listen to me ramble on about becoming a Mastermind.

Let's go inside the International League of Masterminds and get you started!

CHARACTER CREATION

Welcome to the International League of Masterminds. Let me introduce you to Mastermind Lord Fredrick Slitherton. You already have met Minion Walter Pantaloons. These fine chaps will show you around and help you become a Mastermind and a Minion. Lord Fredrick can be a bit of a character at times but don't mind him. I think he got off the wrong side of the horse today. Walter here is one mighty fine Minion who can give you some tips on getting toolbelt items.

Before you begin you will need a character sheet or piece of paper and a writing utensil. Once you are ready you should mosey on down to the end of the hallway and through the double wooden doors. Ya'll don't forget to look at the portraits along the wall. My portrait is the 29th on the left. They are some of the finest Masterminds that have ever lived. Some day you might be posing for your own portrait. Someday, if you're clever and strong and smart. Best of luck to ya'll.

MASTERMIND CHARACTER CREATION

Fellow Masterminds! McCoy has told me that you need some...help taking over the world.

Take it from me, Mastermind Lord Fredrick Slitherton, it all comes down to execution. You will need to get the Minions help, even though I think they're fairly useless. But not everyone can be an evil Mastermind like myself with this stylish curly mustache and black cape. The way to conquer the world is to complete your master plan or what I like to call a 'project'.

Every triumphant master plan has three basic steps. You will build upon each step successively, as you can't reach step 3 if you haven't completed step 1. Hopefully you already knew that. If not, then we have some other issues to work on, but I digress.

Before we discuss your project, let us talk about you and who you are. Every Mastermind needs a name. A really good name - something memorable that rolls off the tongue. Something that will make your Minions cry out in cheers whenever you succeed or what they'll say to beg for your mercy when they fail you and your clearly awesome plan. What should we call you?

If you need some help, which I know you probably do, here is a list of names I have come up with.

Write it down on the 'Character Sheet' in front of you, next to the word 'Mastermind' as that is what you should be calling yourself.

Once you have done that we can continue to the more important aspects of being a Mastermind.

MASTERMIND NAMES

Mastermind Zoe Pumpernickel, Doctor of
    Veterinary Medicine.

Windy Drawers

Mastermind Norbidingle Goldfoot

Professor Amelia Elke Whompturtle, Ph.D
    Neurochemistry and Marine Biology

Mastermind Gloom, Lord of Sadness

Mastermind Rings Espenbrenner III

Mastermind PhantasmaVictoria

Mastermind Frogbear Robot

Mastermind Archdruid Beorn

Jorb Hagaren Chooser of the Pink Rhombus

Mastermind: Professor Demigauss

Mastermind Sebastian Tristan Aristotle Benedict
    Bonaparte Yamamoto *aka Mr. Stabby*

Mastermind Sir Corben Smoots

Mastermind Lee "Gobbo" Forge

Mastermind Captain Xavier Purplebeard of the
    Pirate Ship Overkill

Dr. Hawktopus

Angelique The Greek

Mastermind Lord Fullbladder, Master of Goblins

Mastermind Baron von Bubblebath

Mastermind Sir Per Fluous, Lord of Point Lesse

The Secret DM

Cyborg Millard Fillmore

Bruce McDeathmaster

The Cuddlebunny… of DEATH

The next step in becoming a Mastermind is to define your best quality. Every Mastermind has a key quality that allows them to accomplish the task at hand.

What makes you a Mastermind?

Everyone is different but you… YOU can take over the world. Perhaps you have the quality to shoot beams from electromagnetic glasses. Or maybe you squish people with your insanely large feet. Write this down below your name. For myself, Mastermind Lord Fredrick Slitherton, I write down 'The most devious grin that sends shivers down your spine'. Write down only one quality right now. Only one I SAY!

As you can see, you're here along with a number of other Masterminds. You may be thinking….'Why are they here? I am the SMARTEST Mastermind in the WORLD! These other Masterminds will just get in my way.'

Well, keep thinking that. You'll get your chance to thwart these other Masterminds. The world only has room for one ruler, after all.

If you were previously a masterful Minion (see page 32) you've been instructed to write down your favorite toolbelt item from a previous challenge as your first quality. Write it in that first spot.

When Kentucky McCoy beat all the other minions to become a Mastermind he decided to take his lasso as his favorite toolbelt item. I don't think this was his best choice but that's just me.

MASTERMIND!
~~MINION~~

Kentucky McCoy

ITEMS

SuperSonic Toaster Oven

Neverending Lasso

Shrink Ray - Medium Size

A Bag of Evil Marbles

The World's Cutest Puppy

Teleporting Car

MY MINION

I see you can somewhat follow directions so let's try and move on to a more complicated task.

Next, take your piece of paper and pass it to the Mastermind on your left. No, really, it will be okay. You'll eventually get it back.

As you receive a piece of paper in front of you, review the name and the qualities listed. Really consider the Mastermind on the paper. Study them. Apply some of that considerable brainpower you have. Write down something about them, some quality or item you observe. I know you may not like to read or write – just know that when you become as amazing as myself you can have an intern do the work for you. Now take a moment to add a new quality to this list in the next blank spot.

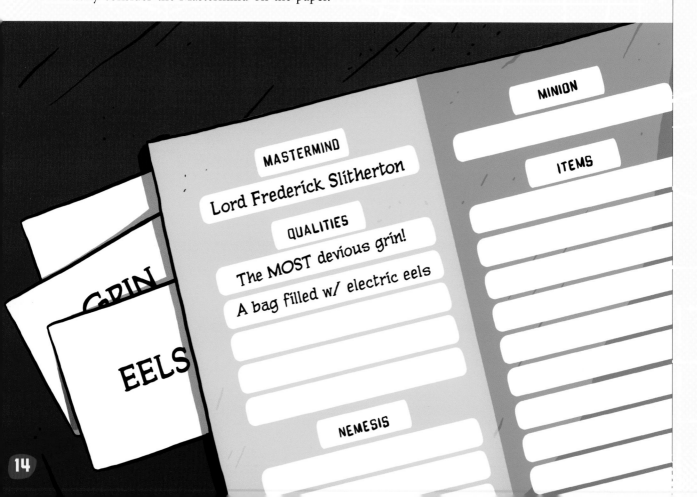

Once you've added a new quality to the list, pass it again to the left. Keep passing to the left until all five slots have been filled. Should you receive your paper back before all the slots are filled, you are to fill them in yourself. You're ready to proceed when you have FIVE (5) qualities listed on your sheet beneath your name.

Nice job! Now it's time to introduce yourselves to the others. Tell everyone your name and who you are. What makes you the Mastermind that you are. Why do you want to take over the world?

The world is your stage, don't be small about this.

MINION

ITEMS

MASTERMIND

Lord Frederick Slitherton

QUALITIES

The MOST devious grin!

A bag filled w/ electric eels

Mind reading goggles

A square jar of peanut butter

A pocket sized foldable bridge

NEMESIS

GRIN

Bridge

Before you continue on it is time to fill out the information about your Nemeses. On the piece of paper there are 3 sections labeled: Round 1, Round 2 and Round 3.

Turn to the person on your right and write down their Mastermind name next to Round 1.

Turn to the 2nd person on your right and write down their Mastermind name next to Round 2.

Finally, turn to the 3rd person on your right and write down their Mastermind name next to Round 3.

To Do List:
Make Gary Pay!!!
Get even with the
Perni
Tacos

GRIN

Bridge

MINION

ITEMS

MASTERMIND
Lord Frederick Slitherton

QUALITIES
The MOST devious grin!
A bag filled w/ electric eels
Mind reading goggles
A square jar of peanut butter
A pocket sized foldable bridge

NEMESIS
Indestructible Gary
ious Smotherer

This reminds me of my Nemesis Dark Baron Harold Sigfried. He had this telekinetic hard hat that could destroy almost anything. But you all know how that ended.... at the bottom of a volcano in Hawaii.

Such a shame really.

No not really, he was kind of an idiot, now that I think about it.

Right, if you could just continue through the brass doors to the next room that would be splendid. I need to go back to my secret lair and take some medicine to bring down my headache.

MINION CHARACTER CREATION

Good afternoon Minions, welcome to basement of the International League of Masterminds. This is where the Union of Minions meet. I know it doesn't look like much but lucky for us we have juice and cookies.

Let me introduce myself. My name is Minion Walter Pantaloons and I have a pretty nifty toolbelt. It's filled with shiny items like my magnetic wand and my lunchbox filled with gummy worms. I really do like shiny objects. Before you are allowed to go out into the world to get your own items and help those Masterminds there's just some super fun paperwork to fill out.

Turn your character sheets to the side that says "MINION". You should write your Minion name after that. I like writing it in big bold letters so everyone can read it. I'm sure you have a lovely name just like mine. If for some reason you don't have a name, I might be able to help you. Somewhere around here is a list. Here it is.

I know it seems silly that I'm wearing this nametag but the Masterminds upstairs have a hard time remembering all of our names. At least the Masterminds gave us toolbelts to hold all our items. A few of you might already have a toolbelt from previous missions. On the little piece of paper there you only have to fill out one toolbelt item. You only get one for now as there have been a few budget cuts.

Once that's done, we'll go around the room to introduce ourselves. I always like meeting new Minions who can be my friends. Then we go to the final presentation before you help conquer the world!

MINION NAMES

Minion George, caster of traps.

Silky Drawers

Minion Froogle the Fearless

Minion: Otto "Stickyfingers" Rogers, Elevated Octopus

Minion Drake, The Sneaky Snake Minion

Lazy Guitar playing Cat Minion

Minion Murray

Penguin Zombie Minion Low Sodium

Minion Deagol

Minion Huei Cleaner of the Bubble

Minion: Van der Bot

Mini-on, the miniature minion

Minion Tohalo

Daryl the Minion of Lee

Monkey Minion Maximillian

iGor

Maia Dow, The Destroyer of Worlds

Minion Kevin, the Intern

Minion Squeaky, the giant Rubber Duck

Marionette Jen Teale

Munchkin

Minionette Clarence

Dakron, The Fabric Minion

Robotic Minion FJ6

GAME CARDS

Masterminds and Minions, I Mastermind Lord Fredrick Slitherton will be presenting to you how to try and go about conquering the world. I stress try because I know that none of you will ever be able to defeat me, but this will at least get you closer, and give me some competition. Competition keeps a Mastermind sharp.

Before we begin the presentation there is another minor task at hand. It's small really, barely worth mentioning. All master plans consist of three steps like I told you when we first met. I have found through my years of being the most diabolical Mastermind there has ever been that I must take risks and develop my plan as I go.

Each of you will contribute 3 cards consisting of a word or short phrase. These words can be anything at all and you will have to win each step of the plan to collect your three-phrase PROJECT.

This may sound like a daunting task but I assure you it isn't. Think about a few outlandish objects or places. The world is your oasis and a good Mastermind can make a plan out of anything. I once had to make a plan using the Pythagorean theorem. That plan didn't work out so well as I had let the Minions calculate the Great pyramid's hypotenuse.

As I was saying, anything can be written on these cards. This task may be a little harder so here is a list of project words for you to ponder over. These project cards will be shuffled once you are done so another Mastermind might get the project card you have written. Dastardly fun isn't it?

Once you have completed this step, collect the cards in a pile and shuffle them. Then place them in the middle of your table face down. Now it is time to begin. The person who speaks up first is the first Mastermind.

SAMPLE WORDS

Ninja
Panda
Tacos
The Eiffel Tower
The Moon
Tambourines with little bells
The London Eye (Ferris Wheel)
Sewers of NYC
Rainbow colored streamers
Calculators
The Great Wall of China
Computer virus
Giant death ray laser
Ant colony
Didgeridoo
The worlds largest planetarium
Global Cheese trading conglomerate
The Olympics
Battle cruiser in Deep Orbit
Oysters
A map of the Marianas Trench
Wall Street
Jumbo jet plane
Mrs Murphy's entire 4th grade class
The world's combiest combover
Really clean ears
Four and a half yards of cape fabric
Highly polished magnets

Top secret soda recipe
Gigantic squid
Golden Dragons
Umbrellas
Turtleneck sweaters

I hope you have been paying attention to Mastermind Lord Fredrick Slitherton. He says some silly things sometimes - especially the part about not wanting our help. He should know that I, Minion Walter Pantaloons, always strive to do my best when helping Masterminds. Here is how you can help the Masterminds succeed in their plans.

After listening intently to both the Mastermind's and Nemesis' plans, each Minion must secretly decide who they want to help. You have two voting tokens in front of you, one color for the Mastermind, and a different color for the Nemesis. Pick up the tokens and privately decide who you want to help, (privately as in no one else can see your choice). Consider the toolbelt items you may receive with your vote.

Remember you can only help one - either the Mastermind or the Nemesis. Choose your token and hold it out in a closed fist and wait for the Mastermind's instructions. When the Mastermind asks you who you are voting for, show your token and describe how you will help using one of your toolbelt items.

I want you to succeed so I shall give you an example!

As Mastermind Lord Fredrick Slitherton asks me who I'm helping I turn over my hand and show my blue token. This means I'm helping the Nemesis. I then say: "I am helping Nemesis Dark Baron Harold Sigfried with my magnetic wand. I shall run around to every tv and warp the picture with my wand!"

I know each of you can do it and I hope you collect many toolbelt items. I better go as Slitherton gets annoyed if I talk for too long.

GAME PLAY: MASTERMIND TURN

As I have told you before, I, Mastermind Lord Fredrick Slitherton never liked getting help from Minions but I found at times some of them could be helpful. You must instruct the Minions to rise up and choose who they will vote for. I find that a bold loud "Minions.... ARISE!" works to get any last minute stragglers to pay attention.

It is imperative that you ask each Minion who they are voting for and how they will help. You don't want a lazy Minion do you? Of course not! Make sure those Minions tell you their reasons!

Once you have asked each and every one of the Minions instruct them to place the tokens in the center of the table. Hopefully they realize to only place the token of the Mastermind they are voting for in the center of the table. You probably will have to keep track of this. They are Minions, you know.

Now listen closely as the next steps are most important. Both the **MASTERMIND** and **NEMESIS**, should pick up four fudge dice and roll them on the table. On your four dice count all the pluses on the table and subtract the minuses. Leave the blanks alone, they do nothing.

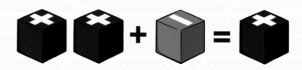

Fudge dice might be new to some of you so I shall explain this a little further. Let's say you roll the 4 dice and get a +, -, +, and a blank. You now have two pluses, one minus, and a blank that we can ignore. Take the two "pluses" and subtract the one "minus" and get a positive one! Very simple for such an evil genius Mastermind! Even a Minion could figure it out.

MASTERMIND, count the number of tokens of your color from the center of the table and add that to the total from the dice.

NEMESIS, count the number of tokens of your color from the center of the table and add that to the total from the dice. Announce to the table with some pride your totals.

The Mastermind with the highest number wins! If there is a tie, should there be a tie, I shall explain how to deal with your failure in a moment.

MASTERMIND! If you have the highest number pick up that first project card and write the word down in the first space next to 'Project'. Thank the Minions for assisting you and remind them of what their new toolbelt item is! You should also tell them to write it down, as they will probably forget.

If you have lost, I suggest you hang your head and try to do better next time.

NEMESIS! If you have the highest number, congratulations! You have thwarted the one person you despise the most. Take the card and turn it over, out of play. Praise the Minions for helping you and award them their new toolbelt item! Hopefully by now, the Minions realize to actually write it down.

A good Mastermind knows that ties can happen at any time. I might have been a little harsh calling it a failure, though it has never happened to me.

Once the Fudge dice and Minion Points are added together if the outcome is a tie, the Mastermind is given a choice.

When describing the plan the Mastermind identified one quality that he used to help with his plan. The Mastermind can choose to cross off this quality (and never use it again) to win the card. The Minions who helped the Mastermind then receive the toolbelt item. If the Mastermind does not wish to get rid of the quality the card is discarded and does not go to the Nemesis. [See page 31 for the ranking chart]

GAME PLAY: ROUNDS

The game is played in three rounds with each player taking a turn as the Mastermind. This means you will be a Mastermind three times. You will also be a nemesis three times. Think of all the plans you can accomplish!

Minions! I suggest listening to the Masterminds as they are smarter and more evil than you. Remember to use your toolbelt when helping with a plan and always cheer loudly when you help a Mastermind succeed. Having more toolbelt items is good for business and the Minion with the most toolbelt items at the end can become a Mastermind of their very own.

Masterminds, now you're ready to conquer the world. Remember there are only 3 rounds of play and once completed you must return to the International League of Masterminds. If you are unable to complete your three-step plan during the 3 rounds I suggest you try your darnedest to stifle the plans of your Nemeses.

At the end of the game you will be asked to count the number of project cards you have completed and the number of qualities remaining. Each card is worth two points and each quality is worth one point. The Mastermind with the most number of points will take over the world. If there is a tie the Mastermind who thwarted the most plans (project cards won as a Nemesis) wins.

Ruling the world takes cunning and decisive plans. Never underestimate your Nemesis and watch out for those Minions.

Go now and try to rule the world, and do not come back until you are finished!

FINISHING THE GAME

THE INTERNATIONAL LEAGUE OF MASTERMINDS

Minions and Masterminds! Please come and sit in the blue leather seats in the auditorium. I think Mastermind Kentucky McCoy helped design the room. I hope that one of the masterminds here has completed their plan to rule the world, but I would like to address the Minions first.

Minions, count the number of tool belt items on your paper. The Minion(s) with the most items has done something that the rest of you have failed at. This Minion should be rewarded for helping so many plans succeed.

As such, I Lord Fredrick Slitherton hereby declares that this Minion from this day forth be a Mastermind. Minion no more!

You will receive your Mastermind pin in the debriefing room later.

Now for the fun part. Masterminds, I know you have tried your hardest but sometimes your hardest just isn't enough. Take a look at your paper. Each card you have won is worth 2 points. Each quality you still have is worth 1 point. Refer to the chart to find where you rank.

The Mastermind with the highest rank has taken over the world!

When two or more Masterminds tie with the same rank the Mastermind with the most Nemesis cards wins. If there is a still a tie the Masterminds end up squabbling like little girls and no one is able to conquer the world. Do you understand?

Remember there can only be one Mastermind to rule the world.

When you are finished please continue on to the debriefing room.

MASTERMIND POINTS AND RANKING CHART

RANK	PROJECT CARDS	QUALITIES	POINTS
1	3 Cards	5 Abilities	11
2	3 Cards	4 Abilities	10
3	3 Cards	3 Abilities	9
4	2 Cards	5 Abilities	9
5	3 Cards	2 Abilities	8
6	2 Cards	4 Abilities	8
7	2 Cards	3 Abilities	7
8	1 Card	5 Abilities	7
9	1 Card	4 Abilities	6

THE DEBRIEFING ROOM

Howdy again! It's me Mastermind Kentucky McCoy. I bet my britches one of you here became a Mastermind today. There is some grub on the table so please help yourself.

I can see ya'll have been very busy trying to take over the world. I would like to begin by congratulating the winning Minion. You must have been quick to the draw to beat everyone else.

Now you must pick your favorite item on your toolbelt. Go on, I know you have a favorite. Once you have done that I must collect your toolbelt as you now get this De-luxe Mastermind pin.

Let's give a big round of applause for our newest Mastermind!

Did any of you Masterminds tie with the same ranking? That never ends well, let me tell you. You just end up squabbling away and wind up at the bottom of a volcano. Hopefully there was a winning Mastermind. If so, then congratulations to you! It is quite an achievement to rule the world. What was the favorite part of your plan? Go on, tell everyone.

It is time to end our journey together. I'd like to ask the winning Mastermind to go through this side door here. You must get ready for your portrait session. As for the rest of you I hope you get some rest around a warm fire. Tomorrow you can try and take over the world again!

ONLINE PLAY

Want even more ways to play Project Ninja Panda Taco? Well you can use the Internet to find some friends to play. Here are a few tips to help with the transition.

SETUP

You can use Google+ Hangouts with video cameras to see and talk to the other Masterminds.

Create 1 Mastermind at a time by asking each player for a quality.

Have 1 person write down all the project cards and hold one up to the camera at the beginning of each turn.

GAME PLAY

Keep track of your qualities and toolbelt items on character sheets in Google documents or printed out at home.

Use an online dice roller or roll Fudge dice off camera.

Use voting tokens or write "Mastermind" and "Nemesis" on a note card to hold up to the camera.

Don't forget to check out the website at *ProjectNPT.com* for more information and helpful web applications you can use!

CLASSROOM PLAY

Want to play PNPT in your classroom? It's as easy! PNPT can be tied to the following Common Core State Standards and will have your kids developing their own Masterminds in now time. Play it as a class with a group of kids controlling each Mastermind, or in a small group setting where each student controls their own. Your students will have a blast creating the story with their classmates and then turning the game into a narrative, a comic book, or a class skit. Look for full lesson plans on *ProjectNPT.com*.

SPEAKING AND LISTENING: COMPREHENSION AND COLLABORATION

CCSS.ELA-Literacy.SL.1 Engage effectively in a range of collaborative discussions (one-on-one, in groups, and teacher-led) with diverse partners on grade level topics and texts, building on others' ideas and expressing their own clearly.

CCSS.ELA-Literacy.SL.1b Follow agreed-upon rules for discussions and carry out assigned roles.

CCSS.ELA-Literacy.SL.1c Pose and respond to specific questions by making comments that contribute to the discussion and elaborate on the remarks of others.

CCSS.ELA-Literacy.SL.3 Summarize the points a speaker makes and explain how each claim is supported by reasons and evidence.

LANGUAGE: CONVENTIONS OF STANDARD ENGLISH

CCSS.ELA-Literacy.L.1 Demonstrate command of the conventions of standard English grammar and usage when writing or speaking.

LANGUAGE: KNOWLEDGE OF LANGUAGE

CCSS.ELA-Literacy.L.3 Use knowledge of language and its conventions when writing, speaking, reading, or listening.

CCSS.ELA-Literacy.L.3a Expand, combine, and reduce sentences for meaning, reader/listener interest, and style.

CCSS.ELA-Literacy.L.3b Compare and contrast the varieties of English (e.g., dialects, registers) used in stories, dramas, or poems.

WRITING: TEXTS, TYPES AND PURPOSES

CCSS.ELA-Literacy.W.3 Write narratives to develop real or imagined experiences or events using effective technique, descriptive details, and clear event sequences.

CCSS.ELA-Literacy.W.3a Orient the reader by establishing a situation and introducing a narrator and/or characters; organize an event sequence that unfolds naturally.

CCSS.ELA-Literacy.W.3b Use narrative techniques, such as dialogue, description, and pacing, to develop experiences and events or show the responses of characters to situations.

CCSS.ELA-Literacy.W.3c Use a variety of transitional words, phrases, and clauses to manage the sequence of events.

CCSS.ELA-Literacy.W.3d Use concrete words and phrases and sensory details to convey experiences and events precisely.

CCSS.ELA-Literacy.W.3e Provide a conclusion that follows from the narrated experiences or events.

KICKSTARTER SUPPORTERS

A very big "Thank you" to all of the backers from Kickstarter.

LEAGUE OF MASTERMINDS

JOHN ROGERS

KEEGAN BATEMAN

TIM RODRIGUEZ

**JIM
RAGGI**

**CLAES
SVENSSON**

**SHARON
TERRILL**

**WILLIAM
WONG**

PROJECT

Jason Ramboz
Peter Griffith
Josh Rensch
Nate Lawrence
Derek Grimm
Robert

MINION UNION 1521

Leo Lalande
Gianluca Casu
Martijn Schenk
Ben Balestra
Nathan Olmstead
Sara Kristman

MASTERMIND

Laura Wong
Kayne Newell
Halsted Larsson
Tim White
Kim Stone
John Mehrholz
Eric Ausley
Sean Belowich
Allen Turner
Michael Wight

ARCHNEMESIS

Jason Slingerland
Dave Chalker
Christopher Mennell
James Priebnow
Tom Cadorette
Heath White
Brennan Taylor
Duane Sibilly
Hans Cummings
Connie M. Allison

TAKEOVER

Tresi Arvizo
Matt Fray
Irven Keppen
Kelsey Paul
Chris Dulsky
Anthony Franchini
Chris Nolen
Candida Norwood
Yoshi Creelman
Michael Kiesling
Patrick Walsh
Elric Chou
Daniel Slater
Lee Langston
Chad Underkoffler
Grady W. Smithey III
Melina Pinilla
Joseph Le May
Cameron Precord
Jen Driver-Sylvia

NEMESIS

Brian Engard
Sven Hannemann
Paco Garcia Jaen
Michael Stackpole
Michael Iachini
Daniel Cetorelli
Angie Wambaugh
Brian Allred
Justin Lance
Christopher Corbett
Miguel Pineiros
Mark Valente
Adam David Pinilla
Martijn Waegemakers
Johnathan L Bingham
David Logan
Eric M. Paquette
Jesse R Davis
Rick Neal
Keith Scholz
Bruce Paulson
Kyle Pauley
Philip Gelatt
Haley Rose
Mark Richardson
Zack Walters
Anna Walker
Matthew Evans

Oren Geshuri
Ken Finlayson
Adrian Stein
Paul A. Catalano, Jr
Jim Sigler
Stephanie Turner
Cerity Mellark

ENHANCED TOOLBELT

Paulo de Tiege
Jeremy Morgan
Brian Benoit
Ernest Flatt
Jonathan Ly Davis
Steven Ness

TOOLBELT

Jamie Chambers
Brian Liberge
Matthew D. Gandy
Matt Forbeck
Chris Perrin
Tim Seiger
David Mihola
Eric Lytle
Curtis Hay
Kat Lim
Jim RyanF
Chris Hearns
Jennifer Skahen
Todd Zircher
Jonathan Campbell
fantomas
MIke Nutt
Scott Gable
Capellan
Kristoffer Lunden
James Macleod
Ben Mund
Kevin Weiser
Dale McCoy, Jr
Kevin Kulp
James Stuart
PK Sullivan
Glenn Seiler

Gail Terman
Paul Drussel
Andy "awmyhr" MyHR
Chris Bernhardi
Michael Kohne
Paris Green
Jose Daniel Campos Alfaro
Benjamin Bangsberg
Andy Kitkowski
Chuck Wendig
David Sowa
Mark Haines
Ben Johnson
Alphonso Butt
Jason King
Brad Johnson
David Bowers
Alden Strock
Ewen Cluney
Steven Furlanetto
Bryan Rennekamp
Rod Cobb
Patty Kirsch
Rafe Ball
Monte Cook
Mark Jacobsen
Maxim Nikolaev
Chris Czerniak
Mark Nunnikhoven

Ian McVicker
Alice Carback
Jim Sweeney
Mark Diaz Truman
Nearly Enough Dice
Andrew Peregrine
Rocha
Lisandro Gaertner
Michael Godesky
Wade Rockett
Marcos Silva
SinCitySnowman
Ian Borchardt
Sarah Williams
Nobilis Reed
Daryl Gubler
Francis Fernandez
nulloperations
Wesley K Hall
Ron Krause
Mats Carlsson
Jocelyn Koehler
Leonard Balsera
Michael Bentley
Clint Weathers
Will Hindmarch
John LeBoeuf-Little
Darren Moser
Sean T. DeLap

Flavio Mortarino
Bret Gillan
Matteo Turini
Lukas Myhan
Clay Karwan
Justin D. Jacobson
gunnergreg
Hans Chung-Otterson
Stew Wilson
David Saggers
Jeffrey Fuller
Jennifer Martin
FelTK
Rochelle Mantanona
Dale Medhurst
Seth Hartley
Shannon Ryke
Mauro Ghibaudo
Robert Ferency-Viars
Eric Stevens
Michael
Chad Stevens
Troy "Wrongtown" Hall
Gilbert Isla
Guy MacDonnell
R.D. Nottingham

MASTERMIND

QUALITIES

NEMESIS

ROUND 1

ROUND 2

ROUND 3

PROJECT

MINIONS ARISE !

MINION

ITEMS

MY MINION

PROJECT NINJA PANDA TACO

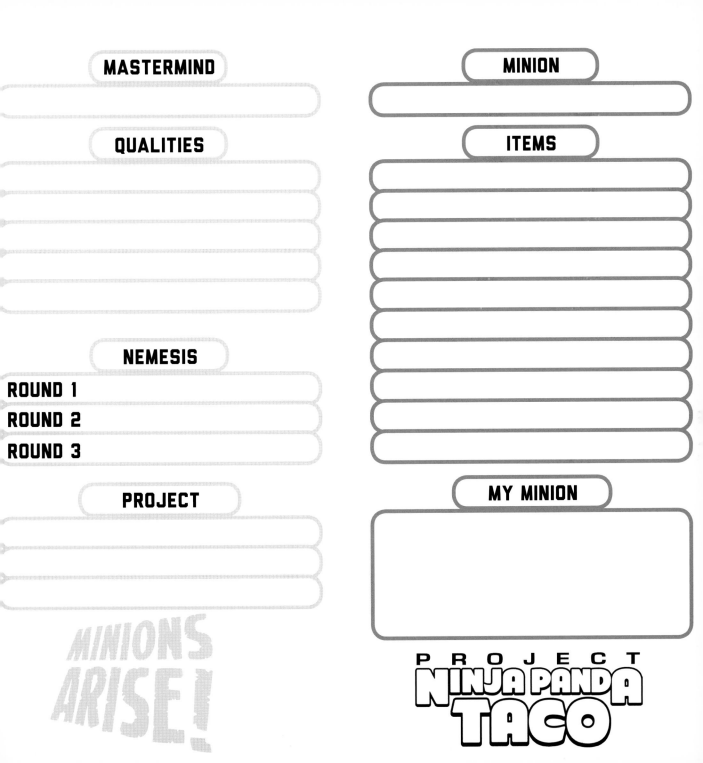

MASTERMIND

QUALITIES

NEMESIS

ROUND 1

ROUND 2

ROUND 3

PROJECT

MINIONS ARISE !

MINION

ITEMS

MY MINION

PROJECT
NINJA PANDA TACO

MAKING MASTERMINDS

What is your Mastermind's Name?

Create 1 Quality for your Mastermind

Pass your sheet to the person on your left

Write 1 Quality for this Mastermind

Repeat process until your sheet is returned

MINION CHARACTER

What is your Minion's Name?

Create 1 Toolbelt for your Mastermind

Draw your Minion!

ASSIGN NEMESES

Turn to the person on your right

Write down their Mastermind Name as Nemesis 1

Turn to the 2nd person on your right

Write down their Mastermind Name as Nemesis 2

Turn to the 3rd person on your right

Write down their Mastermind Name as Nemesis 3

PROJECT CARDS

Write 3 cards each with a word or phrase

Shuffle everyone's cards

Place cards face-down in the center of the table

PLAYING THE GAME

The first player will play their Mastermind Character

The Mastermind reads off their first Nemesis

The other players will play their Minion Characters

1 MASTERMIND TURN

Turn over the top Project Card

Using one of your qualities, describe the next sequential step of your plan

Persuade the Minions to help you by offering a new Toolbelt Item

Ask the Nemesis how he will stop you!

2 NEMESIS TURN

Using one of your qualities, describe how you will stop the Mastermind's plan

Persuade the Minions to help you by offering a new Toolbelt Item

3 MINION TURN

Vote for the Mastermind or the Nemesis

Describe how you will help using your Toolbelt Item

4 ROLL!

Mastermind and Nemesis roll 4 fudge dice

Add Minion votes

Highest roll wins

5 WINNER

Mastermind writes word as project, helping minions get promised Toolbelt Item

Nemesis keeps card, helping minions get promise toolbelt item

MASTERMIND TURN

Turn over the top Project Card

Using one of your qualities, describe the next sequential step of your plan

Persuade the Minions to help you by offering a new Toolbelt Item

Ask the Nemesis how he will stop you!

NEMESIS TURN

Using one of your qualities, describe how you will stop the Mastermind's plan

Persuade the Minions to help you by offering a new Toolbelt Item

PROJECT

NINJA PANDA TACO

WINNER

Mastermind writes word as project, helping minions get promised Toolbelt Item

Nemesis keeps card, helping minions get promise toolbelt item

ROLL!

Mastermind and Nemesis roll 4 fudge dice

Add Minion votes

Highest roll wins

MINION TURN

Vote for the Mastermind or the Nemesis

Describe how you will help using your Toolbelt Item